# Would You Rather...

## CHALLENGE GAME

# EASTER

# Introduction

There is nothing more fun for my family than asking Would You Rather... questions to each other. We could be in the car, going for a walk or just sitting around the dinner table. The idea for this book came up after my son had received yet another joke book for his birthday. "Dad," he said, "I wish there was a good Would You Rather... book out there." So my son, Robbie age 9, my daughter Aubriana age 13 and my wife Carrie decided one day to write our own.

Not only was it a fun family activity to come up with the questions, but it was even more fun to hear how everyone responded. Would Your Rather... investigations are a great way to spark conversation and get to know the people close to you a little better.

We hope you enjoy our first book of Would You Rather... Easter Edition questions as you celebrate the holiday with friends and family.

# Would Your Rather . . .
# Game Rules

## 2 Players

1. One person reads a question from the book.
2. The other person answers the question with their reason.
3. The person reading the question answers as well with their reason.
4. Trade off asking each other questions back and forth.
5. Enjoy each other's company.
6. Don't forget to have fun!

## 2 or more Players

*Game Objective*
Be the person with best reasoning as judged by the group.

*Game Setup*
1. Try and sit in a circular formation.
2. Choose a person to be the judge for the first round.

# Would Your Rather ...
# Game Rules

*How to play?*

1. The judge chooses a question from the book.
2. The judge may decide to go in order or skip around.
3. Players respond to the question starting with the person to the left of the judge.
4. After each person has a turn, the judge decides which answer is best and why.
5. That person receives a point on the score sheet.
6. The new judge becomes the player to the left.
7. Keep playing until someone wins five points.


*Challenge Version*

1. Use sticky notes or paper.
2. Instead of answering out loud, the players write down their answer choice with their reason on a piece of paper.  They give it to the judge.
3. The judge scrambles the answers and reads them out loud.
4. Everyone gets to vote on their favorite.
5. The winner of the round is the one who gets the most votes.
6. If there is a tie then all players get a point.
7. Play until a person wins five points.

## Have Fun!

# Score Sheet

| Game | | Game | | Game | |
|---|---|---|---|---|---|
| Player Name | Game Points | Player Name | Game Points | Player Name | Game Points |
| | | | | | |
| | | | | | |
| | | | | | |
| | | | | | |
| | | | | | |
| | | | | | |
| | | | | | |
| | | | | | |

| Game | | Game | | Game | |
|---|---|---|---|---|---|
| Player Name | Game Points | Player Name | Game Points | Player Name | Game Points |
| | | | | | |
| | | | | | |
| | | | | | |
| | | | | | |
| | | | | | |
| | | | | | |
| | | | | | |
| | | | | | |

# Score Sheet

| Game | | Game | | Game | |
|---|---|---|---|---|---|
| Player Name | Game Points | Player Name | Game Points | Player Name | Game Points |
| | | | | | |
| | | | | | |
| | | | | | |
| | | | | | |
| | | | | | |
| | | | | | |
| | | | | | |
| | | | | | |

| Game | | Game | | Game | |
|---|---|---|---|---|---|
| Player Name | Game Points | Player Name | Game Points | Player Name | Game Points |
| | | | | | |
| | | | | | |
| | | | | | |
| | | | | | |
| | | | | | |
| | | | | | |
| | | | | | |
| | | | | | |

# Score Sheet

| Game | | Game | | Game | |
|---|---|---|---|---|---|
| Player Name | Game Points | Player Name | Game Points | Player Name | Game Points |
| | | | | | |
| | | | | | |
| | | | | | |
| | | | | | |
| | | | | | |
| | | | | | |
| | | | | | |
| | | | | | |

| Game | | Game | | Game | |
|---|---|---|---|---|---|
| Player Name | Game Points | Player Name | Game Points | Player Name | Game Points |
| | | | | | |
| | | | | | |
| | | | | | |
| | | | | | |
| | | | | | |
| | | | | | |
| | | | | | |
| | | | | | |

# Score Sheet

| Game | | Game | | Game | |
|---|---|---|---|---|---|
| Player Name | Game Points | Player Name | Game Points | Player Name | Game Points |
| | | | | | |
| | | | | | |
| | | | | | |
| | | | | | |
| | | | | | |
| | | | | | |
| | | | | | |
| | | | | | |

| Game | | Game | | Game | |
|---|---|---|---|---|---|
| Player Name | Game Points | Player Name | Game Points | Player Name | Game Points |
| | | | | | |
| | | | | | |
| | | | | | |
| | | | | | |
| | | | | | |
| | | | | | |
| | | | | | |
| | | | | | |

# Score Sheet

| Game | | Game | | Game | |
|---|---|---|---|---|---|
| Player Name | Game Points | Player Name | Game Points | Player Name | Game Points |
| | | | | | |
| | | | | | |
| | | | | | |
| | | | | | |
| | | | | | |
| | | | | | |
| | | | | | |
| | | | | | |

| Game | | Game | | Game | |
|---|---|---|---|---|---|
| Player Name | Game Points | Player Name | Game Points | Player Name | Game Points |
| | | | | | |
| | | | | | |
| | | | | | |
| | | | | | |
| | | | | | |
| | | | | | |
| | | | | | |
| | | | | | |

# Would you rather . . .

eat chocolate cake

## or

chocolate pudding for an Easter dessert?

# Would you rather ...

look for 100 eggs that are easy to find

**or**

25 eggs that are hard to find?

 **TERRIBLE TASTEBUD TEST ALERT!**

# Would you rather . . .

*eat a jelly bean that tastes like pencil shavings*

## Or

*a jelly bean that tastes like mushrooms?*

# Would you rather ...

*have pretty flowers that smelled bad*

**or**

*ugly flowers that smelled nice?*

# Would you rather ...

*have Easter candy that had raisins in it*

## or

*Easter candy that had nuts in it?*

# Would you rather ...

play a video game about a bunny that hides eggs

**or**

an app about a duck that hides bread?

# Would you rather ...

celebrate Easter in Sweden

Or

Jamaica?

# Would you rather . . .

play in April
showers

 **or**

pick May
flowers?

# Would you rather ...

hear the song
"Here Comes
Peter Cottontail"
played on a guitar

**or**

a piano?

# Would you rather ...

celebrate Easter at the White House

**or**

a fun house?

# Would you rather ...

*randomly turn into a rabbit for a day once a month*

**or**

*randomly turn into a duck for a day once a month?*

# Would you rather . . .

go to the park

**or**

go to a birthday party on the first day of spring?

# Would you rather ...

pet one bunny 100 times

 **or**

*100 bunnies just one time each?*

 **TERRIBLE TASTEBUD TEST ALERT!**

# Would you rather ...

eat a jelly bean that tastes like fish scales **Or**

 a jelly bean that tastes like cat breath?

# Would you rather . . .

*jump far like a rabbit*

**or**

*glide on water like a duck?*

# Would you rather . . .

have a baby chick
that could sing
songs

**or**

tell jokes?

# Would you rather ...

*have eyes that change color*

  **or**

*hair that changes color depending on the Easter color you think?*

# Would you rather . . .

be completely
bald

**or**

have rabbit fur for
hair?

# Would you rather . . .

*hunt for eggs at the bottom of the ocean*

**or**

*at a playground?*

# Would you rather ...

have spring for the entire year

**or**

fall for the entire year?

# Would you rather . . .

search for Easter eggs at a museum

 **or**

a pizza parlor?

# Would you rather ...

*own a chocolate factory*

**or**

*a bicycle factory?*

# Would you rather ...

have an Easter Unicorn

**or**

an Easter Bigfoot if the Easter Bunny had to retire?

# Would you rather ...

be in an Easter bunny costume with shoes too tight

**or**

a head too big?

# Would you rather . . .

*invent an egg dance*

**Or**

Don't be shy, share it with the group!

*an egg handshake?*

# Would you rather ...

read a book about
a rabbit that could
play basketball

**or**

a duck that
entered a singing
competition?

# Would you rather ...

have an Easter basket made of gold

 **or**

receive a year supply of the candy of your choice?

# Would you rather ...

celebrate Easter
in March

 **or**

*April?*

# Would you rather . . .

find eggs with a friend

**or**

by yourself?

# Would you rather ...

celebrate Easter
five years in the
past

**or**

five years in the
future?

# Would you rather ...

make Easter
decorations

 **or**

Halloween
decorations?

# Would you rather ...

have pancakes

 **or**

bacon for Easter breakfast?

 **TERRIBLE TASTEBUD TEST ALERT!**

# Would you rather ...

*eat a jelly bean that tastes like expired milk*

## or

 *a jelly bean that tastes like sausage surprise?*

# Would you rather . . .

celebrate Easter
on the Amazon
River

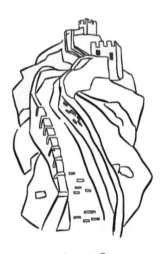

**or**

at the Great Wall
of China?

# Would you rather ...

*start a new Easter tradition*

**or**

*end one that already exists?*

# Would you rather ...

travel to school in an egg-shaped spaceship

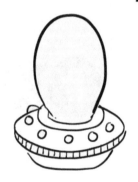

**or**

with special rabbit boots that could jump 50 feet?

# Would you rather ...

*search for Easter eggs in the snow*

**or**

*in the sand?*

# Would you rather ...

crack 1000 eggs

**or**

pick 1000 flowers?

# Would you rather ...

have duck feet

or

rabbit ears?

# TERRIBLE TASTEBUD TEST ALERT!

# Would you rather ...

eat a jelly bean that tastes like sweaty socks

## or

a jelly bean that tastes like worms?

# Would you rather ...

*have your first name be Rabbit*

## or

*Hare?*

# Would you rather . . .

*have a job growing flowers*

**or**

*delivering flowers?*

# Would you rather ...

*be in a pool of marshmallows*

**or**

*a pool of chocolate?*

# Would you rather ...

hunt for Easter eggs on the back of a giraffe

or

an elephant?

# Would you rather ...

watch an Easter
parade

**or**

be in an Easter
parade?

 TERRIBLE TASTEBUD
TEST ALERT!

# Would you rather ...

eat a jelly bean that tastes like grass

**Or**

 a jelly bean that tastes like burnt toast?

# Would you rather . . .

*dye 100 eggs*

**or**

*hide 100 eggs?*

# Would you rather ...

hunt for eggs in
the morning

**or**

*the afternoon?*

# Would you rather ...

*wear pink socks*

**or**

*purple shoes?*

# Would you rather ...

*only drink hot chocolate*

**or**

*chocolate milkshakes for the rest of your life?*

# Would you rather ...

*receive plastic eggs that are filled with actual coins*

**or**

*chocolate coins?*

# Would you rather ...

*have an Easter basket that could change colors*

**or**

*one that could sing you to sleep each night?*

# Would you rather ...

*have a bucket full of jelly beans*

## or

*a backpack full of chocolate bars?*

 **TERRIBLE TASTEBUD TEST ALERT!**

# Would you rather ...

eat a jelly bean that tastes like bath water **Or**

 a jelly bean that tastes like raw shrimp?

# Would you rather ...

give up Spring Break for an extended summer vacation

## or

give up a week of summer vacation for an extended Spring Break?

# Would you rather . . .

use a baseball bat to hit uncooked eggs

**or**

hard-boiled eggs?

# Would you rather . . .

*stir tubs of liquid chocolate*

**or**

*wrap chocolate eggs in foil as your full time job?*

# Would you rather ...

only be able to eat white chocolate

 **or**

dark chocolate for the rest of your life?

# Would you rather ...

*tiptoe through the tulips*

**or**

leap through the
lilies?

# Would you rather ...

*play paintball*

**or**

*laser tag at an Easter party?*

 **TERRIBLE TASTEBUD TEST ALERT!**

# Would you rather ...

*eat a jelly bean that tastes like blue cheese*

**Or**

 *a jelly bean that tastes like turkey and gravy?*

# Would you rather ...

be a candy taste tester

**or**

a candy new flavor creator?

# Would you rather ...

prepare all the materials for egg dyeing

 **or**

would you rather clean everything up afterwards?

# Would you rather ...

sleep on Easter basket grass

**or**

on a pile of leaves?

# Would you rather ...

sing an Easter song in front of a crowd of

people

**or**

Don't be shy, share it with the group!

dance an Easter dance in front of a crowd of people?

# Would you rather ...

get to name a
new candy bar

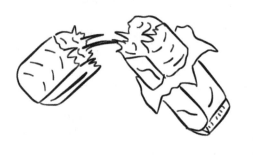 **or**

a new crayon
color?

# Would you rather ...

taste the best chocolate in the world

taste the best peanut butter cookie in the world?

# Would you rather . . .

make an Easter donation to a food pantry

**or**

an animal shelter?

# Would you rather ...

spend Easter in an apartment in a big city

**or**

a house in the country?

# Would you rather . . .

babysit baby chicks

or

baby ducks?

# Would you rather . . .

*always have to wear your Easter best clothes*

## Or

*always have to wear your pajamas?*

 TERRIBLE TASTEBUD
TEST ALERT!

# Would you rather ...

*eat a jelly bean that tastes like coffee grounds*

## OR

*a jelly bean that tastes like dandelions?*

# Would you rather ...

decorate eggs with markers

**or**

paints?

# Would you rather . . .

have a remote control Easter basket

**or**

one that would pick up things for you?

# Would you rather ...

read a news article about the history of chocolate

 **or**

how different countries celebrate Easter?

# TERRIBLE TASTEBUD TEST ALERT!

## Would you rather . . .

eat a jelly bean that tastes like a library book

# Or

a jelly bean that tastes like earwax?

# Would you rather . . .

*always have to hop everywhere*

# or

*always have to waddle everywhere?*

# Would you rather ...

take an Easter hot
air balloon ride

**or**

an Easter African
safari tour?

# Would you rather ...

each candy with a spoon

 **or**

a fork if you couldn't use your hands?

# Would you rather . . .

paint a picture of flowers

 **or**

rabbits?

# Would you rather . . .

have your favorite movie star

## or

your favorite singer over for Easter dinner?

# Would you rather ...

*have your birthday on Easter*

**or**

*Halloween?*

# Would you rather ...

wear an Easter bonnet

 **or**

a straw hat with flowers on it?

# Would you rather . . .

celebrate Easter
on a boat

**or**

*in a camper?*

# Would you rather . . .

*have jelly beans filled with grape jelly*

**or**

*strawberry jelly?*

# Would you rather ...

see what Easter celebrations were like 100 years ago

**or**

100 years into the future?

# Would you rather ...

go hunting for eggs on a skateboard

**or**

on a bicycle?

# TERRIBLE TASTEBUD TEST ALERT!

# Would you rather ...

eat a jelly bean that tastes like dog food

## or

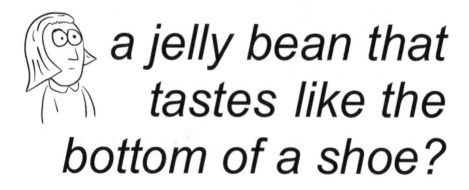

a jelly bean that tastes like the bottom of a shoe?

# Would you rather ...

*get a new jacket*

**or**

*a new pair of shoes for Easter?*

# Would you rather . . .

have green dye on your fingers for 10 days

 **or**

purple dye on your ears for five days?

# Would you rather ...

see the world's largest Easter basket

**Or**

the world's tiniest Easter basket?

# Would you rather ...

walk barefoot on broken eggshells

**or**

barefoot on hot sand?

# Would you rather ...

*celebrate Easter with a TV star*

**or**

*a president?*

# Would you rather ...

go out in public
dressed as a
rabbit

**or**

a baby chick?

# Would you rather ...

*have to smell rotten eggs for three hours a day*

**or**

*never smell anything ever again?*

# Would you rather ...

be able to talk to rabbits and ducks and have them understand you, but you can't understand them

 **or**

would you rather be able to understand what rabbits and ducks say but they can't understand you?

# Would you rather ...

*go for an Easter drive in a convertible*

**or**

*a dune buggy?*

# Would you rather ...

wash your hair
with a raw egg

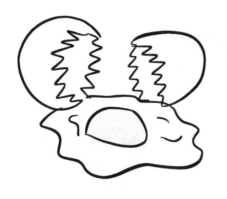 **or**

wash your hair
with chocolate
sauce?

# Would you rather ...

have a new candy bar named after you

**or**

a newly discovered bird named after you?

# Would you rather . . .

have a conversation with the Easter Bunny

or

the Tooth Fairy?

 **TERRIBLE TASTEBUD TEST ALERT!**

# Would you rather ...

eat a jelly bean that tastes like pond water

**Or**

 a jelly bean that tastes like laundry soap?

# Thanks For playing!